MW00532121

Rah! Rah! Ramen

by Sara Childs

Interactive Direct Publishing
New York

Manufactured in the United States of America.

ISBN-digital edition: 978-0-9898036-1-8

Print edition
ISBN-10: 0989803635
ISBN-13: 978-0-9898036-3-2

Sara Childs is a pseudonym of Interactive Direct

Book design by Piet Halberstadt

interactivedirect.net

Dedicated to Isobel

So she doesn't starve at school

I Love Ramen!!!

Ramen is a staple in American student cuisine. If you're a full-time college student, money and time are major issues. Ramen is cheap and with a microwave oven super fast to prepare.

Ramen is high in carbohydrates and if you use the flavor packet, fat and sodium. BUT... the up side is, ramen has fewer calories than many fast foods. Ramen is less expensive and using a microwave oven is faster than standing in line and ordering fast food burger. Ramen has almost half the calories of a popular fast food chicken sandwich, less than a third of the calories of a reuben sandwich. Ramen has less than a quarter of the fat and a third of the calories of deep fried xcrispy chicken tenders.

But ramen noodles can be more than a super fast microwavable carbohydrate meal. If you discard the flavor packet, add a can of stewed tomatoes, some Italian herbs, powdered garlic and dried onion flakes you've created Ramen Marinara in 5 to 7 minutes or try Ramen in Red Clam Sauce, the prep and cooking time is 7 to 10 minutes.

Ramen is one of the cheapest foods in the supermarket and with imagination can be a versatile staple in your college cuisine. RAH! RAH! RAMEN recipes will add flavor and variety to a super fast, super cheap meal.

Sara

You And Your Micro

Microwave cooking is convenient and fast, but special care should be taken when cooking or reheating food. The wattage of your microwave oven will determine the cooking time, the higher the wattage/power level the faster the cooking time. To find the power level check the inside of the oven or the back of the unit where the serial number is listed. The higher the wattage, the faster it will cook food.

Use microwave-safe bowls, cups and utensils. Cover the bowls with microwave-safe lids or wraps. Do not overfill the bowl; leave enough space between the food and the wrap, don't let the food touch the wrap, this can cause leaching of chemicals from the wrap to the food. The moist heat will promote cooking and destroy harmful bacteria, but leave a corner of the lid or wrap uncovered to allow steam to vent,

A microwave oven cooks less evenly than a conventional oven. Microwaves penetrate food to a depth of 1 to 1 1/2 inches creating cold spots in the center. Always stir and rotate the food midway through the time to eliminate cold spots and to ensure even cooking. If your microwave oven has a turntable, you should still stir the food from the outside of the bowl to the center, from the top to bottom.

Always allow standing time, the cooking process continues and is completed during this time.

Use extreme caution when unwrapping and serving reheated or cooked food, Remove the wrap away from you to avoid the hot steam.

Cooking Utensils

USE:

Oven-proof glass measuring cups (2 and 4 cups)
   Pyrex or Anchor Hocking

Oven-proof ceramic Corning Ware

White paper plates and towels

Wax paper, microwave-safe wrap (Glad Wrap)

Measuring spoons

A sharp knife

A can opener

DO NOT USE:

Empty yogurt or cheese containers

Insulated cups or bowls

Metal wraps, pans, utensils anything with metal

Earthen wear bowls or cups or ceramic dinner wear with
   metallic paint

You And Your Ramen Cuisine

(OR NOSH, CHOW, GRUB WHATEVER) Ramen is tasty and filling, but can get old pretty quick. One of the ways to quickly transform a bowl of ramen noodles is by adding a condiment or sauce that won't break the bank. This is a list of 16 inexpensive items that can add an infinite variety to your ramen cuisine. These items will last for months and take up a minimal amount of space.

Your Pantry
A bottle of dried Italian Herbs #1
Dried parsley
Powdered garlic
Dried onion flakes
Flour #2
Olive oil
Parmesan cheese (grated)
Bacos
Capers #3
Sriracha Sauce #4
Hoisin Sauce #5
Oyster Sauce #6
Soy Sauce #7
Candied ginger or powdered ginger
Peanut butter (creamy)
Toasted Sesame Oil #8
Ziplock bags to store leftovers

1. Italian Herbs, a bottle of dried Italian Herbs should be a mixture of Thyme, Rosemary, Sage, Oregano, and Basil.

2. Flour, Wondra is flour in a convenient storage container

3. Capers are the flower buds of Capparis spinosa. They are dried, then pickled in a brine of vinegar, wine and salt. The flavor is tangy and lemony. Nonpareil is the smallest variety from the South of France and is very expensive. Larger capers are stronger in flavor and less aromatic and less expensive.

4. Sriracha Sauce is a hot sauce made from a combination of chili peppers, distilled vinegar, garlic, sugar, and salt.

5. Hoisin Sauce is commonly known as Chinese barbecue sauce is sweet and salty sauce made with soy sauce, red chilies, garlic, vinegar and sugar.

6. Oyster Sauce is condiment made from sugar, salt, oyster essence and water thickened with cornstarch.

7. Soy Sauce is a condiment made from a fermented soybeans, roasted grain and brine. Every Asian country has it's own form of soy sauce, we recommend Japanese soy sauce, it's not as salty.

8. Toasted Sesame Oil is a nutty flavored polyunsaturated vegetable oil made from toasted sesame seeds

The addition of vegetables, eggs, cheese, peanut butter or a can of tuna fish you can have a balanced healthy meal prepared in a few minutes. Adding a simple garnish; slicing fresh scallions or zesting and slicing a lemon can brighten your taste buds. How your ramen looks and smells will affect how you enjoy your meal.

With a well stocked pantry most of these recipes take a maximum of 5 minutes of prep time and 7 minutes of cooking and standing time. Imagine, 12 minutes for a filling healthy meal, less time than waiting in line for a fast food hamburger and cheaper then an Reuben sandwich.

Contents

You And Your Micro 4
Cooking Utensils 5
You And Your Ramen Cuisine 6
Ramen Alfredo 11
Ramen With Garlic & Butter 13
Ramen Marinara 15
Italian Egg Drop Soup 17
Ramen With Fresh Tomatoes 19
Ramen Primavera 21
Ramen In Red Clam Sauce 23
Ramen In White Clam Sauce 25
Ramen Frittata 27
Ramen In Arrabbiata Sauce 31
Pasta Ponza 33
Veggie Medley 35
Ramen With Pesto & Peas 37
Spinach Cannellini Ramen Soup 39
Minestrone Soup 41
Cannellini Tomato Soup 43
Pesto Soup 45
Tuscan Ramen Soup 47
Tuna Ramen 49
Macmen N' Cheese 51
Tuna Casserole 53
Summer Ramen 55
Ramen With Bacos & Edamame 57
Veggie (Vegetarian) Ramen 59
Greek Ramen 61
Lemon, Cannellini & Capers Ramen 63
Greek Egg Drop Soup 65
Burrito Bowl 67
South West Tacos 69
Beef With Broc 71
Dan Dan Ramen 73
Chop Suey 75
Vegamen 77
Chowramen 79
Tomato Beef Ramen 81
Ramen With Snow Peas & Water Chestnuts 83
Peanut Ramen 85
Udon Ramen With Poached Egg 87
Hot N' Sour Ramen 89
California Egg Drop Soup 93
Udon With Beef Jerky 95
Ramen With Edamame 97
Tamago Udon Ramen 99
Pad Thai Ramen 101
Pad Thai Ramen With Tofu 103
Red Curry Soup 105
Tai Curry Ramen 109
2 Egg Drop Soup 111
Chocolate Ramen 113
Strawberry Delite 115
Coconut Banana Pudding 117
Lemon Curd Ramen 119

Ramen Alfredo

1 package of ramen (discard the flavor packet)
2/3 cup + 1 tablespoon water
1/4 cup of Half & Half (or 4 containers from the cafeteria)
1/4 teaspoon salt
A pinch of pepper
1 teaspoon flour
1/2 cup frozen peas*
1 tablespoon butter (2 pads from the cafeteria)
1 tablespoon Parmesan

Combine the Half & Half and water, mix and set aside.

Rinse the peas in cold water to remove the frost, do not defrost and set aside.

In a microwaveable bowl break the ramen sheets in half, you will end up with 4 pieces, sprinkle the ramen with flour, add salt, a pinch of pepper. Pour the Half & Half mixture over the ramen, make sure all the ramen has been coated with the mixture. Cover the bowl with microwave-safe wrap and microwave for 2 minutes, remove the bowl from the oven, uncover the bowl, (reserve the wrap) with 2 forks separate the ramen into strands, add the peas and butter, carefully mix to incorporate. Recover the bowl and microwave for 80 seconds. Remove the bowl from the oven, DO NOT UNCOVER THE BOWL, let stand, covered for 3 to 5 minutes. Uncover and serve.

Garnish with Parmesan.

*Reseal the bag of frozen peas, secure with a rubber band to keep excess moisture out, reserve for use in Ramen with Pesto and Peas.

Ramen With Garlic & Butter

1 package of ramen (discard the flavor packet)
2/3 cup water
1/2 teaspoon powdered garlic
1 teaspoon olive oil
1/4 teaspoon salt
1 tablespoon butter (2 pads from the cafeteria)
Parmesan cheese

Combine the water, garlic powder, olive oil and salt, mix well and set aside.

Place the ramen in microwaveable bowl, break the ramen sheets in half, you will end up with 4 pieces. Pour the water mixture over the ramen, make sure all the ramen has been coated with the mixture. Cover the bowl with microwave-safe wrap and microwave for 2 minutes. Remove and unwrap the bowl (reserve the wrap), with 2 forks separate the strands of noodles, add the butter, mix well. Recover and microwave for 1 minute. Remove the bowl from the oven, DO NOT UNCOVER, let stand for 3 to 5 minutes. Uncover and serve.

Garnish with Parmesan.

Ramen Marinara

1 package of ramen (discard the flavor packet)
3/4 cup canned chopped tomatoes*
1/2 cup water
1/4 teaspoon garlic powder
1 teaspoon olive oil
1/2 teaspoon dried parsley
1 teaspoon sugar (1 packet from the cafeteria)

Combine the chopped tomatoes with water, garlic powder, dried parsley, sugar and olive oil, mix well and set aside.

Place the ramen in microwaveable bowl, break the ramen sheets in half, you will end up with 4 pieces. Pour the tomato mixture over the ramen, make sure all the ramen has been coated with the mixture. Cover the bowl with microwave-safe wrap and microwave for 2 minutes. Remove the bowl from oven, unwrap the bowl (reserve the wrap), with 2 forks separate the ramen into strands, mix in the tomatoes to incorporate. Recover the bowl and microwave for 90 seconds. Remove the bowl from oven, DO NOT UNCOVER, let stand for 3 to 5 minutes. Uncover the bowl and toss to mix.

Garnish with Parmesan.

*Seal the tomatoes in a zip-lock bag. Reserve for use in California Egg Drop Soup or Ramen Primavera. Do not store longer than 3 days.

Italian Egg Drop Soup

1 package of chicken ramen
1 1/2 cups water
1/2 flavor packet
1/2 cup frozen peas thawed (run frozen peas under
    cold water)*
2 eggs (beaten)
2 tablespoons Parmesan cheese

Combine the water and 1/2 of the flavor packet, mix well and set aside. (if you want more soup add more water).

In a small bowl or cup using a fork beat eggs till frothy, set aside.

Place the ramen in microwaveable bowl, break the ramen sheets in half, you will end up with 4 pieces. Pour the reserved water mixture over the ramen, make sure all the ramen has been coated with the mixture. Cover the bowl with microwave-safe wrap and microwave for 3 minutes. Remove the bowl and unwrap the bowl (reserve the wrap), with 2 forks separate the strands of noodles, add peas, gently stir the soup, add the eggs a tablespoon at a time, DO NOT MIX, recover the bowl and microwave for 2 minutes. Remove the soup from the oven, DO NOT UNCOVER THE BOWL, let the bowl stand for 2 minutes. Uncover and serve.

Serve with a sprinkling of Parmesan

*•Reseal the bag of peas, keep excess moisture out. Reserve for
  use in Ramen Alfredo or Ramen With White Clam Sauce.*

Ramen With Fresh Tomatoes

1 package of ramen (discard the flavor packet)
2/3 cup water
2 coarsely chopped plumb tomatoes
1 teaspoon olive oil
1/4 teaspoon garlic powder
1 tablespoon dried onion
1/2 teaspoon dried Italian herbs
1/4 teaspoon sugar
Salt and pepper
1 tablespoon Parmesan cheese (optional)
1 teaspoon dried parsley

Combine the water, tomatoes, olive oil, garlic powder, onion, Italian herbs and sugar, mix well, and set aside.

Place the ramen in microwaveable bowl, break the ramen sheets in half, you will end up with 4 pieces. Pour the reserved mixture over the ramen, make sure all the ramen has been coated with the water mixture. Cover the bowl with microwave-safe wrap and microwave for 2 minute. Remove and unwrap the bowl (reserve the wrap), with 2 forks separate the ramen into strands. Recover the bowl and microwave for 90 seconds. Remove the bowl from oven, DO NOT UNCOVER, let the bowl stand for 2 minutes. Uncover, add salt and pepper to taste and serve.

Garnish with Parmesan and parsley

Ramen Primavera

1 package of ramen, (discard the flavor packet)
1 1/2 cups of frozen Italian vegetables*
1 teaspoon olive oil
1/2 cup water
1 cup canned chopped tomatoes**
1/2 teaspoon dried parsley
1 tablespoon dried onions
1 tablespoon Parmesan
Salt and pepper to taste

Place the vegetables and olive oil in a microwave proof bowl, cover with microwave-safe wrap, microwave for 2 minutes. Remove the bowl from oven, remove the wrap (reserve the wrap) stir the veggies, recover the bowl and set aside.

Combine the water, tomatoes, onions and parsley, mix well and set aside.

Place the ramen in microwaveable bowl, break the ramen sheets in half, you will end up with 4 pieces. Pour the water mixture over the ramen, make sure all the ramen has been coated. Cover the bowl with microwave-safe wrap, microwave 2 minutes, remove the bowl from the oven and unwrap (reserve the wrap) use 2 forks to separate the strands of noodles. Add the vegetables, microwave for 90 seconds. Remove the bowl from the oven, DO NOT UNCOVER, let the bowl stand for 2 minutes. Uncover and serve.

Top with Parmesan.

*Reseal the bag of frozen vegetables, keep frozen and reserve to use in Tuscan Vegetable Soup
**Seal the tomatoes in a zip-lock bag, store refrigerated for up to 4 days. Reserve for use in Ramen Marinara, Ramen Primavera or California Egg Drop Soup.

Ramen In Red Clam Sauce

1 package of ramen, (discard the flavor packet)
1 can (12 oz) stewed tomatoes
1 can (4 oz) of clams (drained, reserve juice)
1 tablespoon olive oil
1/4 cup reserved clam juice
1/4 teaspoon Italian mixed herbs
1/2 teaspoon dried parsley

Combine the stewed tomatoes, reserved clam juice, Italian herbs, parsley and olive oil and set aside.

In a microwaveable bowl, break the ramen sheets in half, you will end up with 4 pieces. Pour tomato mixture over noodles, make sure all the ramen is coated. Cover the bowl with microwave-safe wrap, microwave for 2 minutes. Unwrap the bowl, (reserve the wrap) and with 2 forks separate the ramen strands. Re-wrap the bowl, microwave for 1 minute, DO NOT UNCOVER, let the bowl stand, covered 2 minutes. Uncover, add the clams, mix well, recover and microwave 30 seconds. Uncover and serve.

Garnish with a sprinkling of parsley.

Ramen In White Clam Sauce

1 package of ramen, (discard the flavor packet)
2 tablespoon of Half & Half (2 take out containers
    from the cafeteria)
1/2 cup reserved clam juice
1/4 cup water
1 teaspoon dried parsley
1 teaspoon flour
1 can (4 oz) of clams (reserve juice)
1/4 teaspoon salt
A pinch of pepper
1 tablespoon butter (2 pads from the cafeteria)
1/4 cup frozen peas*

Combine the Half & Half with the reserved clam juice, parsley, salt, pepper and water and set aside.

Rinse peas in cold water to remove frost, do not defrost.

In a microwaveable bowl, break the ramen sheets in half, you will end up with 4 pieces. Sprinkle the ramen with flour, add salt, a pinch of pepper. Pour the Half & Half mixture over the noodles, make sure all the ramen is coated. Cover the bowl with microwave-safe wrap, microwave for 2 minutes. Unwrap the bowl, (reserve the wrap), with 2 forks separate the ramen strands, add the butter and peas, recover the bowl and microwave for 1 minute. Remove the bowl from the oven, add the clams, mix well, recover the bowl and micro-wave for 30 seconds, remove the bowl from the oven, DO NOT UNCOVER THE BOWL, and let stand for 2 minutes. Uncover and serve.

Garnish with a sprinkling of parsley.

*Reseal the bag of frozen peas, keep frozen and reserve to use in Ramen Pesto or Italian Egg Drop Soup.

Ramen Frittata

1 package of ramen
3/4 cup water
1 cup frozen peas*or canned asparagus
1/2 cup chopped frozen spinach**
1 egg beaten well
1/4 cup Monterey Jack*** or Cheddar cheeses
1 tablespoon bacos****
Salt and pepper
*1 tablespoon butter more for buttering deep dish (2 pads
from the cafeteria)*
Chopped fresh parsley (optional)

Butter a standard take-out microwaveable dish, 5 1/2 inch
x 2 inch deep, (make sure it's NOT Styrofoam or aluminum.)

In a small bowl add the frozen peas, run cold water over peas
till they are not a solid mass, do not defrost and set aside (if
using canned asparagus, drain, chop and set aside). Run cold
water over frozen spinach, squeeze dry and set aside.

In a bowl beat the egg until frothy, add the cheese, bacos,
salt, pepper, mix well and set aside

In a microwave-safe bowl, break the ramen sheets in half,
you will end up with 4 pieces. Pour 3/4 cup of water over the
ramen, make sure all the ramen has been coated. Cover the
bowl with microwave-safe wrap, microwave for 2 minutes,
remove the bowl from the oven. Unwrap (reserve the wrap)
with 2 forks separate the ramen strands. Recover the bowl
and microwave for 1 minute, remove the bowl from the oven,
DO NOT UNCOVER, let the bowl stand for 3 minutes.

WITH PEAS

Uncover the bowl add the peas and spinach, mix to incorporate, pour egg mixture over noodles. Gently pour mixture
into the buttered container. Cover with microwave-safe wrap,
microwave for 3 minutes. Remove the bowl from the oven,
DO NOT UNCOVER, let the frittata stand, for 3 minutes. $\rightarrow$

WITH ASPARAGUS

Place asparagus in the bottom of the buttered container and set aside. Add spinach to the egg mixture, mix well. Pour egg mixture over noodles, mix to incorporate. Gently scoop mixture on top of the asparagus. Cover with microwave-safe wrap, microwave for 3 minutes. Remove the bowl from the oven, DO NOT UNCOVER, let the frittata stand, for 3 minutes. Uncover and serve.

TO PLATE, place plate over container and flip over. Garnish with chopped parsley.

*Store the frozen peas in a zip-lock bag, keep frozen for use in Pesto or Italian Egg Drop Soup with tofu.
**Store the frozen spinach in a zip-lock bag, keep frozen for use in Cannelloni Ramen Soup or Greek Egg Drop Soup
***Wrap the cheese and store to use in Burrito Bowl or South West Tacos
****Use the bacos in Ramen with Bacos and Edamame

Ramen In Arrabbiata Sauce

1 package of ramen (discard the flavor packet)
1/2 cup water
1 teaspoon olive oil
1/4 teaspoon powered garlic
2 teaspoon dried onion flakes
1/2 teaspoon red pepper flakes* (or 1/2 teaspoon Sriracha)
1/2 teaspoon parsley
1 cup drained chopped tomato**
1 teaspoon Parmesan cheese

Combine the water, olive oil, dried onion, garlic, parsley, and red pepper flakes, mix well and set aside.

In a microwave-safe bowl, break the ramen sheets in half, you will end up with 4 pieces. Pour the water mixture over the ramen, make sure all the ramen has been coated. Cover the bowl with microwave-safe wrap, microwave for 2 minutes, remove the bowl from the oven. Unwrap the bowl, (reserve the wrap) with 2 forks separate the ramen strands. Pour the chopped tomatoes over the ramen, mix to incorporate, recover the bowl and microwave for 2 minutes. Remove the bowl from oven, DO NOT UNCOVER, let the bowl stand for 3 minutes. Uncover, Pour into serving bowl and sprinkle with Parmesan cheese.

*Red pepper flaks can be used in Spinach Cannellini Soup and in all Italian dishes and on pizza.
**Save the left-over tomatoes in a zip-lock bag, do not store longer than 4 days. Reserve for use in Ramen Marinara or California Egg Drop Soup.

Pasta Ponza

1 package of ramen (discard the flavor packet)
1/2 cup water
1/4 cup juice from the can of diced tomatoes
1 tablespoon olive oil
1 teaspoon parsley
1 tablespoon dried onion flakes
1 tablespoon bread crumbs (or day old bread, coarsely crumbled)
2 tablespoon Parmesan
1 cup canned chopped tomatoes*
Parsley and Parmesan

Combine the water, juice from drained tomatoes, olive oil, parsley and onion, mix well and set aside.

Combine the bread crumbs and cheese, mix well and set aside.

In a microwave-safe bowl, break-up ramen sheets into 2 inch pieces. Pour the water mixture over the ramen, make sure all the ramen has been coated. Cover the bowl with micro-wave-safe wrap, microwave for 2 minutes, remove the bowl from the oven. Unwrap the bowl, (reserve the wrap) with 2 forks separate the ramen strands, add the chopped toma-toes, recover, microwave 90 seconds. Remove the bowl from the oven, DO NOT UNCOVER, let the bowl stand 2 minutes. Uncover, use 2 forks to fluff up the pasta, let cool, add bread crumb mixture and mix to incorporate, do not over mix.

Serve with a sprinkling of parsley and Parmesan.

*Seal the tomatoes in a zip-lock bag. Reserve for use in South West Ramen or Ramen Primavera.

Veggie Medley

1 package chicken ramen
1/2 cup water
1 teaspoon olive oil
1/2 flavor packet
1 tablespoon dried onion
1/4 teaspoon garlic
1/2 teaspoon Italian herbs
1 1/2 cup frozen Italian vegetables*
Salt and pepper to taste

Combine the water, olive oil, 1/2 of the flavor packet, the dried onion, garlic and Italian herbs, mix well and set aside.

Run cold water over frozen veggies to remove surface frost, do not defrost. Set aside.

In a microwave-safe bowl, break the ramen sheets in half, you will end up with 4 pieces. Pour the water mixture over the ramen, make sure all the ramen has been coated. Cover the bowl with microwave-safe wrap, microwave for 2 minutes, remove the bowl from the oven, unwrap the bowl, (reserve the wrap) with 2 forks separate the ramen strands. Add the veggies, stir to incorporate, recover the bowl, microwave 90 seconds. Remove the bowl from the oven, DO NOT UNCOVER, let the bowl stand for 2 minutes, uncover, add salt and pepper to taste.

Plate and serve with a sprinkling of Parmesan.

*Reseal the bag of frozen Italian vegetables, keep frozen and reserve to use in Veggie Ramen Soup

Ramen With Pesto & Peas

1 package of ramen, (discard the flavor packet)
1/2 cup water
1 teaspoon olive oil
1 cup frozen peas*
3 tablespoon bottled pesto**
1 teaspoon Parmesan

Combine the water and olive oil, mix well and set aside

Run water over peas to remove surface frost and set aside.

In a microwave-safe bowl, break the ramen sheets in half, you will end up with 4 pieces. Pour the water mixture over the ramen, make sure all the ramen has been coated. Cover the bowl with microwave-safe wrap, microwave for 2 minutes, remove the bowl from the oven, remove the wrap, (reserve the wrap) with 2 forks separate the ramen strands. Add the peas, gradually add the pesto, mix to incorporate, do not over mix, recover the bowl, microwave 90 seconds. Remove the bowl from the oven, DO NOT UNCOVER, let the bowl stand for 3 minutes. Uncover and serve.

Garnish with Parmesan.

*Reseal the bag of frozen peas, keep frozen and reserve to use in Italian Egg Drop Soup.
**Left-over can be used in Pesto Soup.

Spinach Cannellini Ramen Soup

1 package chicken ramen
1/2 flavor packet
1 1/2 cup water
1 tablespoon diced dried onion
1/4 teaspoon garlic
1/4 teaspoon Italian herbs
1/4 red pepper flakes
1 cup cannellini beans*canned (drained and rinsed)
1/2 cup frozen whole leaf spinach**
2 tablespoon Parmesan cheese (optional)

Combine the water, 1/2 of the flavor packet, the dried onion, garlic, Italian herbs and red pepper flakes, mix well and set aside.

Run water over the spinach, squeeze dry and set aside.

In a microwave-safe bowl, break the ramen sheets in half, you will end up with 4 pieces. Pour the reserved water mixture over the ramen, make sure all the ramen has been coated. Cover the bowl with microwave-safe wrap, microwave for 3 minutes, remove the bowl from the oven, remove the wrap, (reserve the wrap) with 2 forks separate the ramen strands. Add cannellini beans and spinach, mix to incorporate. Recover the bowl and microwave for 2 minutes. Remove the bowl from oven, DO NOT UNCOVER, let the bowl stand for 2 minutes. Uncover, pour into a serving bowl, sprinkle with Parmesan cheese, gently mix to combine.

*Store the left-over cannellini beans in a zip-lock bag, refrigerate, do not store longer than 3 days. The beans can be used in Pesto Soup, Lemon, Cannellini and Capers Ramen or Cannellini Tomato Soup.
**Reseal the bag of frozen spinach, secure with rubber band to keep excess moisture out. The spinach can be used in Greek egg drop soup or Frittata.

Minestrone Soup

1 package Chicken ramen
1 cup water
1/2 flavor packet
1/4 teaspoon garlic
1 teaspoon dried parsley
1/2 teaspoon mixed Italian herbs
1 tablespoon dried onion flakes
1/2 cup juice from drained chopped tomatoes
1 cup of canned chopped tomatoes*
1 1/2 cup of left-over vegetables** (cannellini beans,
    kidney beans and frozen vegetables)

Drain and rinse the beans and set aside.

*Run cold water over the frozen vegetables, do not defrost
and set aside.*

Combine the water, 1/2 of the flavor packet, the garlic,
parsley, Italian herbs, onion flakes and reserved tomato juice,
mix well and set aside.

In a microwave-safe bowl, break the ramen sheets in half,
you will end up with 4 pieces. Pour the reserved water
mixture over the ramen, make sure all the ramen has been
coated. Cover the bowl with microwave-safe wrap, microwave for 3 minutes, remove the bowl from the oven, remove
the wrap, (reserve the wrap) with 2 forks separate the ramen
strands. Add cannellini beans, kidney beans, frozen vegetables and chopped tomatoes, mix well. Recover microwave 90 seconds. Remove the bowl from the oven, DO NOT
UNCOVER, let the bowl stand 3 minutes. Uncover and serve.

This soup can go from oven to table if a microwave-safe
bowl is used.

**Seal the tomatoes in a zip-lock bag, store refrigerated for up
to 4 days. Reserve the tomatoes for use in Ramen Marinara,
Ramen Primavera or California Egg Drop Soup.*
***Use an assortment of frozen vegetables and reserved beans
to fill 1 1/2 to 2 cups.*

Cannellini Tomato Soup

1 package chicken ramen
1 1/2 cup water
1/2 flavor packet
1/8 teaspoon powdered garlic
1 tablespoon dried onion flakes
1 teaspoon parsley
1 cup cannellini beans*
1/2 of a 14. 5 ounce can of diced tomatoes**
1 teaspoon Parmesan (optional)
Sprinkling of parsley

Combine the water, 1/2 of the flavor packet, the garlic powder, onion and parsley, mix well and set aside.

Drain and rinse the cannellini beans and set aside.

In a microwave-safe bowl, break the ramen sheets in half, you will end up with 4 pieces. Pour the water mixture over the ramen, make sure all the ramen has been coated. Cover the bowl with microwave-safe wrap, microwave for 3 minutes, remove the bowl from the oven, remove the wrap, (reserve the wrap) with 2 forks separate the ramen strands. Add cannellini beans and tomatoes, mix to incorporate, re-wrap the bowl and microwave for 2 minutes. Remove the bowl from the oven, DO NOT UNCOVER, let the bowl stand 2 to 3 minutes. Uncover, add salt and pepper to taste.

Serve with a sprinkling of Parmesan and parsley.

*Store the left-over cannellini beans in a zip-lock bag, refrigerate, do not store longer than 3 days. Reserve for use in Pesto soup or Lemon, Cannellini and Capers Ramen.
**Seal the tomatoes in a zip-lock bag, store refrigerated for up to 4 days, reserve for use in Ramen Primavera or California Egg Drop Soup.

Pesto Soup

1 package of chicken ramen
1/2 chicken flavor packet
1 1/2 cup water
1 tablespoon store bought pesto*
2/3 cup cannellini beans**
Parsley

Combine the water and 1/2 of the flavor packet, mix well and set aside.

Rinse the cannellini beans in cold water and set aside.

In a microwave-safe bowl, break the ramen sheets in half, you will end up with 4 pieces. Pour the water mixture over the ramen, make sure all the ramen has been coated. Cover the bowl with microwave-safe wrap, microwave for 3 minutes, remove the bowl from the oven, uncover, (reserve the wrap) with 2 forks separate the ramen strands. Add the pesto and cannellini beans, mix well. Recover the bowl, microwave 90 seconds. Remove the bowl from the oven, DO NOT UNCOVER, let the bowl stand 2 minutes. Uncover and serve.

Garnish with parsley.

*Use Pesto in Ramen with Pesto and Peas.
**Store left-over cannellini beans in a zip-lock bag, refrigerate, do not store longer than 3 days, can be used in Lemon, Cannellini and Capers Ramen.

Tuscan Ramen Soup

1 package of ramen, (discard the flavor packet)
1 1/2 cup water
2 tablespoon catchup (or use 4 packets from the cafeteria)
1 tablespoon dried onion flakes
1/4 teaspoon garlic powder
1/4 teaspoon dried Italian herbs
1 teaspoon olive oil
1 cup frozen Italian vegetables*
1/2 cup canned chopped tomatoes**
1 teaspoon Parmesan

Combine the water and catchup, mix well, making sure the catchup is totally dissolved, add onion, garlic, Italian herbs and olive oil, stir to incorporate and set aside.

Rinse the frozen vegetables to remove the frost, do not defrost the vegetables.

In a microwave-safe bowl, break the ramen sheets into 2 inch pieces. Pour the water mixture over the ramen, make sure all the ramen has been coated. Cover the bowl with microwave-safe wrap, microwave for 3 minutes, remove the bowl from the oven, uncover the bowl, (reserve the wrap) with 2 forks separate the ramen strands. Add the chopped tomatoes and veggies, mix to incorporate. Recover the bowl and microwave for 2 minutes. Remove the bowl from the oven, DO NOT UNCOVER, let the bowl stand 2 to 3 minutes. Uncover and serve.

The finishing touch, garnish with Parmesan. Enjoy!

*Reseal the bag of frozen Italian vegetables, keep frozen and reserve to use in Ramen Primavera.
**Seal the tomatoes in a zip-lock bag, store refrigerated for up to 4 days, reserve for use in Ramen Marinara, Ramen Primavera or California Egg Drop Soup

Tuna Ramen

1 package of ramen, (discard the flavor packet)
1/2 cup water
1 teaspoon olive oil
1/4 teaspoon garlic
1 tablespoon dried onion flakes
1 teaspoon parsley
1 cup frozen mixed vegetables*
1 can tuna in oil, drained and broken up into small chunks
1 tablespoon capers**
Salt and pepper

Combine the water, olive oil, garlic, parsley and onion, mix well and set aside.

Microwave the vegetables in a small container for 30 seconds, uncover, stir and set aside.

In a microwave-safe bowl, break-up ramen sheets into 2 inch pieces. Pour the water mixture over the ramen, make sure all the ramen has been coated. Cover the bowl with micro-wave-safe wrap, microwave for 2 minutes, remove the bowl from the oven, uncover the bowl, (reserve the wrap) with 2 forks separate the ramen strands. Add vegetables mix to incorporate, recover and microwave 90 seconds. DO NOT UNCOVER, let the bowl stand 2 minutes, Uncover add tuna, capers, salt and pepper to taste, carefully mix to incorporate.

Garnish with a little parsley.

*Reseal the bag of frozen mixed vegetables, keep frozen and reserve to use in Tuscan Ramen or Vegetable Ramen Soup.
**Use the Capers in Summer Ramen or Lemon, Cannellini and Capers Ramen.

Macmen N' Cheese

1 Package ramen (discard the flavor packet)
1/2 cup water
1/4 cup Half & Half (4 take-out containers from the cafeteria)
1/4 teaspoon hot sauce
1 tablespoon dried onion flakes
1 tablespoon butter (2 take-out pads of butter from the cafeteria)
1/4 cup cheese (Kraft shredded Cheddar, Monterey Jack mix)
1/4 cup sharp cheddar cheese (I used x-sharp white cheddar)
2 tablespoons Bacos (optional)

Combine the water, Half & Half, hot sauce and dried onion flakes. Mix well and set aside.

In a bowl crumble the cheddar cheese (white or yellow) and combine with the reserved Kraft cheese mix. Mix well and set aside.

In a microwave safe bowl, break up ramen into 1 inch pieces. Pour the water mixture over the ramen; make sure all the ramen has been coated. Cover the bowl with micro-wave-safe wrap, microwave 2 minutes, remove the bowl and unwrap the bowl, (reserve the wrap) with 2 forks separate the strands of ramen, add the bacos, recover the bowl and microwave 1 minute, remove the bowl DO NOT UNCOVER, and let stand foe 2 minutes. Uncover the bowl, add the butter and cheese mix to incorporate, do not over mix.

Serve in a bowl and top with toasted breadcrumbs (optional).

TOASTED BREAD CRUMB TOPPING (OPTIONAL)

1 tablespoon + 1 teaspoon breadcrumbs
1 1/2 teaspoons of butter (1 take-out pad of butter the your cafeteria)

Prep the Bread Crumbs

Combine the bread crumbs with the butter in a shallow micro-wave safe bowl. Microwave 30 seconds, remove the bowl from the oven, stir to incorporate, microwave 30 seconds, remove the bowl from oven, stir to make sure the bread crumbs are browning evenly, microwave an additional 10 seconds. Remove the bowl from the oven, stir the bread crumbs and set aside.

Tuna Casserole

1 Package ramen (discard the flavor packet)
1/2 cup water
1/4 cup Half & Half (4 take-out containers from your cafeteria)
1 tablespoon dried onion flakes
1 tablespoon flour
1 tablespoon butter (2 take-out pads of butter from your cafeteria)
1 cup frozen peas*
1 can (4 ounces) of water packed tuna
Salt and pepper
Chopped parsley (optional)

Combine the water, Half & Half and onion, mix well and set aside.

In a small bowl run cold water over peas to remove frost, do not defrost and set aside.

In a microwave-safe bowl, break up the ramen into 1 inch pieces. Sprinkle flour over the ramen, pour the water mixture over the ramen; make sure all the ramen has been coated. Cover the bowl with microwave-safe wrap, microwave 2 minutes, remove the bowl from the oven and unwrap the bowl, (reserve the wrap) with 2 forks separate the strands of ramen. Add the butter and peas, recover the bowl and microwave 90 seconds, remove the bowl from the oven, DO NOT UNCOVER and let stand for 2 minutes. Uncover the bowl, (reserve the wrap) add the tuna, mix well, recover the bowl and microwave 1 minute. Uncover, mix and plate.

Serve topped with parsley.

*Reseal the bag of frozen peas for later use in Ramen with Pesto and Peas.

Summer Ramen

1 package of ramen (discard the flavor packet)
1/2 cup water
1/4 teaspoon garlic
1 teaspoon olive oil
1/2 can of a 14.5 ounce can of diced tomatoes*
1 tablespoon capers** (drained)
1/2 teaspoon parsley

Combine the water, garlic and olive oil and set aside.

Drain the tomatoes, add parsley and capers mix to incorporate, set aside.

In a microwave-safe bowl, break the ramen sheets in half, you will end up with 4 pieces. Pour the water mixture over the ramen, make sure all the ramen has been coated. Cover the bowl with microwave-safe wrap, microwave for 2 minutes, remove the bowl from the oven. Unwrap the bowl, (reserve the wrap) with 2 forks separate the ramen strands. Add tomato mixture, mix well. Recover the bowl, microwave 90 seconds. Remove the bowl from the oven, DO NOT UNCOVER, let the bowl stand 3 minutes. Uncover and serve.

Top with a sprinkling of parsley.

*Seal the tomatoes in a zip-lock bag, store refrigerated for up to 4 days. Reserve for use in Cannellini Tomato Soup, Ramen Primavera or California Egg Drop Soup.
**Use the capers in Tuna Ramen or Lemon, Cannellini and Capers Ramen.

Ramen With Bacos & Edamame

1 package of ramen (discard the flavor packet)
2/3 cup water
1 teaspoon olive oil
1 tablespoon dried onion flakes
1/4 teaspoon powdered garlic
2 tablespoon bacos*
1 cup shelled edamame** beans (frozen or fresh beans)
1 tablespoon Parmesan cheese or parsley

Combine the water, olive oil, onion and garlic, mix well and set aside.

In a small container run water over the edamame to remove frost, DO NOT DEFROST and set aside.

In a microwave-safe bowl, break the ramen sheets in half, you will end up with 4 pieces. Pour the water mixture over the ramen, make sure all the ramen has been coated. Cover the bowl with microwave-safe wrap, microwave for 2 minutes, remove the bowl from the oven. Unwrap the bowl, (reserve the wrap) with 2 forks separate the ramen strands. Add the bacos and edamame, stir to combine, re-wrap the bowl, microwave 90 seconds. Remove the bowl from the oven, DO NOT UNCOVER, let the bowl stand for 3 minutes. Uncover and serve.

Garnish with Parmesan or chopped parsley.

*The Bacos can be use in Frittata or in pasta dishes or salads.
**Reseal the bag of frozen edamame, keep frozen and reserve to use in Ramen with Edamame.

Veggie (Vegetarian) Ramen

1 package of ramen (discard the flavor packet)
1 1/2 cup water
1 teaspoon olive oil
1 tablespoon dried onion
1/4 teaspoon powdered garlic
1/2 teaspoon Italian herbs
1 teaspoon parsley
1/4 teaspoon sriracha sauce
1 teaspoon lemon juice
2 cup frozen mixed vegetables*
Parsley

Combine the water, olive oil, onion, garlic, Italian herbs, parsley, sriracha sauce and lemon juice, mix well and set aside.

Rinse the vegetables in cold water to remove frost, do not defrost and set aside.

In a microwave-safe bowl, break the ramen sheets in half, you will end up with 4 pieces. Pour the water mixture over the ramen, make sure all the ramen has been coated. Cover the bowl with microwave-safe wrap, microwave for 3 minutes. Remove the bowl from the oven, remove the wrap, (reserve the wrap) with 2 forks separate the ramen strands, add the vegetables, recover the bowl and microwave 90 seconds. Remove the bowl from the oven, DO NOT UNCOVER, let the bowl stand 2 to 3 minutes. Uncover and serve.

Top with a sprinkling of parsley.

*Reseal the bag of frozen mixed vegetables, keep frozen and reserve to use in Tuscan Ramen or Ramen Primavera.

Greek Ramen

1 package of ramen (discard the flavor packet)
1 can chopped tomatoes* (or 2 fresh plumb tomatoes chopped)
1/2 cup water
1/4 teaspoon garlic powder
1/2 teaspoon dried Italian herbs
1 teaspoon olive oil
8 coarsely chopped calamata olives**
1 tablespoon capers***

Combine the water, garlic, chopped tomatoes, Italian herbs and olive oil mix well and set aside.

Place the ramen in microwave-safe bowl. Break the ramen sheets in half, you will end up with 4 pieces. Pour the water mixture over ramen, make sure all the ramen has been coated with the mixture. Cover the bowl with microwave-safe wrap and microwave for 2 minutes. Remove the bowl and unwrap, (reserve the wrap) with 2 forks separate the ramen strands and mix well. Recover the bowl and microwave for 90 seconds. Remove the bowl from oven, DO NOT UNCOVER, let the bowl stand for 3 minutes. Uncover, add olives and capers, mix well and serve.

*Seal the left-over tomatoes in a zip-lock bag, refrigerate, do not store longer than 4 days. Reserve for use in California Egg Drop Soup or Ramen Marinara.
**Use the olives in Tuna Ramen or Summer Ramen
***Use the capers in Lemon, Cannellini & Capers Ramen.

Lemon, Cannellini & Capers Ramen

1 package of ramen, (discard the flavor packet)
2/3 cup water
1/4 teaspoon garlic
1 tablespoon olive oil
1 lemon rind sliced
2 + tablespoon lemon juice
1 cup cannellini beans* (drained and rinsed)
1 teaspoon parsley
1 tablespoon capers**
Salt and pepper to taste
1 teaspoon freshly chopped parsley (optional)

Combine the water, garlic and olive oil and set aside.

Wash the lemon, with a peeler, peel the rind from the lemon top to bottom, avoid taking too much of the pith. Slice rind into 1/8 inch wide, long strips, set aside.

In a microwave-safe bowl, break the ramen sheets in half, you will end up with 4 pieces. Pour the water mixture over the ramen, make sure all the ramen has been coated. Cover the bowl with microwave-safe wrap, microwave for 2 minutes, remove the bowl from the oven. Unwrap the bowl, (reserve the wrap) with 2 forks separate the ramen strands. Add cannellini, lemon juice, lemon peel and parsley, recover and microwave 90 seconds. Remove the bowl from the oven, DO NOT UNCOVER, let the bowl stand for 2 minutes, Uncover, add capers, toss to incorporate.

Serve with a sprinkling of parsley and sliced lemon.

*Store the left-over cannellini beans in a zip-lock bag, refrigerate,
do not store longer than 3 days, can be used in Pesto Soup or Cannellini & Tomato Soup.
**Use the capers in Tuna Ramen or Summer Ramen.

Greek Egg Drop Soup

1 package Chicken flavor ramen
1 1/4 cup water
1/2 flavor packet
1 tablespoon lemon
1/2 cup frozen chopped or whole spinach*
    (or 1 cup fresh spinach into 1/4 in strips)
1 egg

Combine the water, 1/2 chicken flavor packet and 1 table-spoon of fresh squeezed lemon juice, set aside.

Run water over the frozen spinach just to remove frost, DO NOT DEFROST or use 1 cup of fresh spinach. Chop the spinach into 1/4 inch thick strips and set aside.

In a small container beat egg till frothy and set aside.

Place the ramen in microwaveable bowl, break the ramen sheets in half, you will end up with 4 pieces. Pour the water/lemon mixture over the ramen, make sure all the ramen has been coated with the mixture. Cover the bowl with micro-wave-safe wrap and microwave for 3 minutes. Remove the bowl from the oven. Unwrap the bowl, (reserve the wrap) with 2 forks separate the ramen strands, stir soup, add spinach and mix well. Recover the bowl and microwave for 1 minute. Remove the bowl from oven. Unwrap and stir, care-fully add beaten egg, 1 tablespoon at a time, do not mix, recover the bowl and microwave for 30 seconds. Remove the bowl from the oven, DO NOT UNCOVER, let the bowl stand for 3 minutes. Uncover and serve.

*Reseal the bag, secure with rubber band to keep excess moisture out, reserve for use in Cannellini spinach ramen.

Burrito Bowl

1 package of ramen (discard the flavor packet)
1/2 cup water
2 tablespoon chili mix
1 tablespoon onion flakes
1/2 cup canned kidney beans*
1 + 1/2 cup of left-over black beans and corn**
1 tablespoon store bought salsa
1/4 cup shredded cheddar or Monterey Jack cheese***
2 tablespoon sliced black olives (optional)

Combine the water, chili mix and dried onions, mix well and set aside.

In a microwaveable bowl break the ramen sheets in half, you should end up with 4 pieces. Pour the chili and water mixture over the ramen, make sure all the ramen has been coated. Cover the bowl with microwave-safe wrap, microwave for 2 minutes. Remove the bowl from the oven, unwrap the bowl, (reserve the wrap), with 2 forks separate the ramen strands. Top the noodles with beans, corn and salsa, recover the bowl with the reserved wrap, microwave for 90 seconds. Remove the bowl from the oven, DO NOT UNCOVER, let the bowl stand for 2 to 3 minutes. Uncover and serve.

Sprinkle with cheese and olives.

*Store the left-over kidney beans in a zip-lock bag, refrigerate, do not store longer than 3 days, use in South West Tacos or Minestrone.
**The left-over black beans should be stored in a zip-lock bag and refrigerated for no longer than 3 days. Left-over corn should be stored in a zip-lock bag and refrigerated for no longer than 3 days. Black beans and corn can be used in South West Tacos.
***The cheese should be wrapped carefully to avoid spoilage. Left-over cup cheddar or Monterey Jack can be used in Ramen Frittata.

South West Tacos

1 package of ramen (discard the flavor packet)
1/2 cup water
1 tablespoon taco mix (such as Old el Paso)
1 tablespoon dried onion
1 teaspoon olive oil
1/2 cup diced tomatoes*
1/2 cup canned corn** (drained)
1/2 cup canned black beans*** (rinsed in cold water)
Old El Paso taco shells

Combine the water, taco seasoning, onion and olive oil, mix well and set aside.

In a microwave-safe bowl, break-up ramen sheets into 2 inch pieces. Pour the taco and water mixture over the ramen, make sure all the ramen has been coated. Cover the bowl with microwave-safe wrap, microwave for 2 minutes, remove the bowl from the oven, uncover (reserve the wrap), with 2 forks separate the ramen strands. Add the chopped tomatoes, mix to incorporate. Recover the bowl and microwave for 90 seconds. Remove the bowl from the oven and let stand, covered, 2 to 3 minutes, let the ramen cool, add the corn and beans, mix to incorporate, but do not over mix.

Scoop taco mixture and carefully fill taco shells.

*Seal the tomatoes in a zip-lock bag, refrigerate, do not store longer than 4 days. Reserve for use in Ramen Marinara or Ramen Primavera.
**Seal the corn in a zip-lock bag, refrigerate, do not store longer than 3 days. Reserve for use in Burrito Bowl.
***Seal the black beans in a zip-lock bag, refrigerate, do not store longer than 3 days. Reserve for use in Burrito Bowl.

Beef With Broc

1 package of ramen (discard the flavor packet)
3/4 cup water
1 tablespoon Hoisin sauce
1 tablespoon dried onion flakes
1/4 teaspoon powdered garlic
1 cup frozen or fresh broccoli*
4 oz beef jerky**
1/4 cup water
Parsley

Break up the beef jerky and soak in 1/4 cup of water for 10 minutes. (the longer the jerky rehydrates the better). Set aside.

Rinse the frozen broccoli to remove the frost, do not defrost, and set aside.

Combine the water and Hoisin sauce mix well, add onion flakes and garlic mix well and set aside.

In a microwave-safe bowl, break the ramen sheets in half, you will end up with 4 pieces. Pour the water mixture over the ramen, make sure all the ramen has been coated. Cover the bowl with microwave-safe wrap, microwave for 2 minutes, remove the bowl from the oven, uncover, (reserve, wrap), with 2 forks separate the ramen strands. Drain the jerky, add the broccoli and jerky to ramen, mix well. Recover the bowl and microwave for 90 seconds. Remove the bowl from the oven, DO NOT UNCOVER, let the bowl stand 2 minutes.

Serve with a sprinkling of parsley.

*Reseal the bag of frozen broccoli, keep frozen and reserve to use in Stir-fry dishes.
**Use the beef jerky in Tomato Beef Ramen or Udon with Beef Jerky.

Dan Dan Ramen
(Shanghai Style Spicy Sesame Noodles)

1 package of ramen (discard the flavor packet)
3/4 cup water
1 heaping tablespoon peanut butter
1/2 teaspoon sriracha sauce
1/4 teaspoon garlic powder
1/2 teaspoon powdered ginger
1 tablespoon soy sauce
1 tablespoon rice wine vinegar
1/4 sesame seed oil
1 teaspoon sugar
3 to 5 tablespoon water
1/4 cup cucumber sliced into thin 3-inch match sticks
2 tablespoon chopped peanuts*
1 tablespoon sesame seeds**

In a small bowl combine the peanut butter, 3 to 5 tablespoons water, sriracha sauce, and mix well. Add garlic, ginger, soy sauce, vinegar, sesame oil, and sugar, mix well and set aside.

In a microwave-safe bowl, break the ramen sheets in half, you will end up with 4 pieces. Pour 3/4 cup water over the ramen, make sure all the ramen has been coated. Cover the bowl with microwave-safe wrap, microwave for 2 minutes. Remove the bowl from the oven, uncover, (reserve the wrap) with 2 forks separate the ramen strands. Recover the bowl, microwave for 90 seconds, remove the bowl from the oven, DO NOT UNCOVER, let the bowl stand covered for 3 minutes. Uncover the bowl, pour peanut mixture over the ramen, mix to incorporate, sprinkle with sesame seeds.

Garnish with cucumber sticks and peanuts.

*The left-over peanuts can be used in Sesame Noodles or Pad Thai as garnish.
**Store the left-over sesame seeds in an air tight container for later use in Sesame Noodles.

Chop Suey

1 package of ramen (discard the flavor packet)
3/4 cup water
1/2 teaspoon sesame oil
1 tablespoons Hoisin sauce
1 tablespoon soy sauce
1 tablespoon dried onions
1/2 teaspoon dried garlic
1/4 sriracha
1 teaspoon cornstarch or flour
1 cup frozen stir fry vegetable*mix
1/4 cup sliced bamboo shoots**
1/4 cup straw mushrooms***
1/4 cup left-over bean sprouts****
Scallions, sliced for garnish

Combine the water, sesame oil, Hoisin sauce, soy sauce, onion, garlic, and sriracha sauce, mix well and set aside.

Run the water over frozen vegetables, do not defrost and set aside.

In a microwave-safe bowl, break the ramen sheets in half, you will end up with 4 pieces. Sprinkle cornstarch or flour over ramen, pour the water mixture over the ramen, make sure all the ramen has been coated. Cover the bowl with microwave-safe wrap, microwave for 2 minutes, remove the bowl from the oven, uncover, (reserve the wrap), with 2 forks separate the ramen strands. Add the vegetables, bamboo shoots, mushrooms and bean sprouts to the bowl, mix to incorporate, recover with wrap, microwave for 2 minutes. Remove the bowl from the oven, DO NOT UNCOVER, let the bowl stand, covered for 3 to 5 minutes. Uncover and serve.

Garnish with sliced scallions.

*Reseal the bag of frozen stir fry vegetables, keep frozen and reserve to use in Vegamen and other Asian dishes
**Store the left-over bamboo shoots in a zip-lock bag, refrigerate, do not store longer than 3 days, use in Pad Thai and other Asian dishes.
***Store the left-over mushrooms in a zip-lock bag, refrigerate, do not store longer than 3 days, use in Hot & Sour Soup or any of the Asian dishes.
****Store the left-over bean sprouts in a zip-lock bag, refrigerate, do not store longer than 3 days, use in Pad Thai.

Vegamen

1 package of ramen (discard the flavor packet)
3/4 cup water
2 tablespoon Hoisin sauce
1 teaspoon soy sauce
1/2 teaspoon sriracha sauce
1/4 sesame oil
1/2 teaspoon ginger or a 1 inch square piece of
   candied ginger sliced into thin strips
1/4 teaspoon garlic
1 teaspoon sugar
1 cup extra firm tofu* sliced into 1/2 inch cubes
1/4 cup canned sliced bamboo shoots**
2 cup frozen stir fry vegetables mix***
sliced scallions

Combine the water, hoisin, soy sauce, sriracha, sesame oil, ginger, garlic and sugar, mix well and set aside.

In a small microwave-safe container microwave the frozen stir-fry vegetables for 1 minute and set aside.

In a microwave-safe bowl, break the ramen sheets in half, you will end up with 4 pieces. Pour the water mixture over the ramen, make sure all the ramen has been coated. Cover the bowl with microwave-safe wrap, microwave for 2 minutes, remove the bowl from the oven, uncover the bowl, (reserve the wrap) with 2 forks separate the ramen strands. Add the tofu, vegetables and bamboo shoots, mix to incorporate, recover the bowl with the reserved wrap, microwave for 2 minutes. Remove the bowl from the oven, DO NOT UNCOVER, let the bowl stand covered for 3 to 5 minutes. Uncover and serve.

Garnish with scallions.

*Store the left-over Tofu in a zip-lock bag, refrigerate, do not store longer than 3 days, use in Pad Thai With Tofu or Udon With Poached Egg.
**Store the left-over bamboo shoots in a zip-lock bag and reserve to use in Chop Suey and Hot and Sour Soup.
***Reseal the bag of frozen stir fry vegetables, keep frozen and reserve to use in Chowramen and other Asian dishes

Chowramen

1 package of ramen (discard the flavor packet)
3/4 cup water
1 teaspoon soy sauce
1/2 teaspoon sesame oil
1/4 teaspoon sriracha sauce
1 tablespoon + 1 teaspoon Hoisin sauce
2 cup frozen stir fry vegetables* (Bird's Eye)
   or left-over frozen veggies
1 egg

In a microwaveable bowl add the vegetables, cover the bowl with microwave-safe wrap, microwave for 1 minute. Unwrap the bowl, (reserve the wrap) stir and recover the bowl and microwave for 45 seconds and set aside.

In a separate container beat the egg until foamy and set aside.

In a cup mix the water, soy sauce, sesame oil with the sriracha sauce and Hoisin sauce, mix well and set aside.

In a large bowl break the ramen sheets in half, you will end up with 4 pieces. Pour soy mixture over the ramen, make sure all the ramen has been coated with the mixture. Cover the bowl with microwave-safe wrap and microwave for 2 minutes. Remove the bowl from the oven, unwrap the bowl, (reserve the wrap) with 2 forks separate the ramen noodles. Add the vegetables, mix to incorporate, recover the bowl and microwave for 1 minute, remove the bowl from the oven, unwrap the bowl, (reserve wrap). Stir the noodles, slowly add the egg by tablespoons, do not mix, the egg should be in a little pocket. Re-wrap the bowl and microwave 30 seconds. Remove the bowl from the oven, DO NOT UNCOVER, let the bowl stand 2 minutes. Uncover and serve.

*Reseal the bag of frozen stir fried vegetables, keep frozen and reserve to use in Chop Suey, Tomato Beef Chowmen and Vegamen.

Tomato Beef Ramen

1 package of ramen, (discard the flavor packet)
2/3 cup water
2 tablespoon catchup
1 tablespoon soy sauce
1 teaspoon sesame oil
1/2 teaspoon powdered ginger or one inch square of candied ginger, sliced thinly
1 plum tomato coarsely chopped or 1/2 cup canned chopped tomatoes***
1 cup frozen stir-fried vegetables**
3 to 4 oz beef jerky*
1/4 cup water
1 teaspoon parsley

Break apart the beef jerky, soak in 1/4 cup water for at least 20 minutes. (the longer, the better)

In a microwave proof bowl add the frozen vegetables, cover the bowl with microwave-safe wrap and microwave for 1 minute. Remove the bowl from the oven, unwrap, (reserve the wrap) stir and add the tomatoes, cover, microwave 30 seconds. Remove the wrap, stir and set aside.

Combine the water, catchup, soy sauce, sesame oil and ginger mix to combine and set aside.

Place the ramen in a microwave-safe bowl, break the ramen sheets in half, you will end up with 4 pieces. Pour the reserved water mixture over the ramen, make sure all the ramen has been coated. Cover the bowl with microwave-safe wrap and microwave for 2 minutes. Remove the bowl and wrap (reserve the wrap), with 2 forks separate the ramen strands. Add meat and vegetable mixture, recover the bowl and microwave for 90 seconds. Remove the bowl from oven, DO NOT UNCOVER THE BOWL, let the mixture stand, covered for 2 minutes. Uncover and serve.

Garnish with parsley.

*Reseal the bag of beef jerky, reserve to use in Udon With Beef.
**Reseal the bag of vegetables, secure with rubber band to keep excess moisture out, reserve to use in Chop Suey or Vegamen.
***Seal the tomatoes in a zip-lock bag. Reserve for use in Ramen Marinara or Ramen Primavera.

Ramen With Snow Peas & Water Chestnuts

1 package of ramen (discard the flavor packet)
1/2 cup water
1 tablespoon oyster sauce*
1 tablespoon dried onion flakes
1/2 teaspoon sesame oil
1 cup snow peas** (fresh or frozen)
1 can (4 oz) sliced water chestnuts (drained)
1 teaspoon chopped or slivered scallions (optional)
1 teaspoon sesame seeds

Combine the water and oyster sauce, mix well, making sure the oyster sauce is dissolved, add the onion and sesame oil, mix and set aside.

Rinse the frozen snow peas to remove the frost, do not defrost and set aside.

In a microwave-safe bowl, break-up the ramen sheets into 2 inch pieces. Pour the water mixture over the ramen, make sure all the ramen has been coated. Cover the bowl with microwave-safe wrap, microwave for 2 minutes. Remove the bowl and uncover, (reserve the wrap) with 2 forks separate the ramen strands. Add the snow peas and water chestnuts to the ramen, mix to incorporate. Recover the bowl and microwave 90 seconds, remove the bowl from the oven, DO NOT UNCOVER, let the bowl stand, covered for 2 to 3 minutes. Uncover and serve.

Garnish with sesame seeds and scallions.

*Use the Oyster Sauce in most Chinese dishes.
**Reseal the bag of frozen snow peas, keep frozen and reserve to use in Chowramen or Tomato Beef Ramen.

Peanut Ramen

SAUCE

2 tablespoon smooth peanut butter*
1 teaspoon soy sauce
1 tablespoon lime juice
1/2 teaspoon sugar
1 teaspoon sesame oil
2 to 4 drops hot sauce or 1/4 teaspoon sriracha sauce
3 to 4 tablespoon water
Scallions and chopped peanuts (optional)

Combine all ingredients, slowly add water to thin sauce to the consistency of applesauce. Mix well and set aside.

RAMEN

1 package of ramen (discard the flavor packet)
2/3 cup water
1 teaspoon sesame seeds

In microwaveable bowl break the ramen sheets in half, you will end up with 4 pieces. Pour the water mixture over the ramen, make sure all the ramen has been coated. Cover the bowl with microwave-safe wrap and microwave for 2 minutes. Remove the bowl and unwrap, (reserve the wrap) with 2 forks separate the ramen strands. Recover the bowl and microwave for 30 seconds. Remove the bowl from the oven, DO NOT UNCOVER, let the bowl stand, covered, for 3 minutes. Uncover the bowl, add sauce, mix to incorporate, do not over mix.

Served garnished with a sprinkling of chopped peanuts and scallions.

*Peanut butter can be used in Pad Thai or Dan Dan ramen recipes.

Udon Ramen With Poached Egg

HOW TO POACH AN EGG

1 egg
1/4 cup water

In a small microwave-safe cup add 1/4 cup of water; carefully break the egg into cup, with a pin carefully prick the yolk in 3 places. A word of caution, if you don't puncture the yoke it will explode! To avoid a mess, and be on the safe side cover the bowl with microwave-safe wrap, leave one corner uncovered to allow steam to escape. Microwave for 1 minute or check every 30 seconds. The egg will be soft boiled. Uncover the bowl and gently drain off the water and set the egg aside.

THE SOUP

1 package Oriental Flavor Ramen
1/2 flavor packet.
1 1/2 cup water
1 tablespoon soy sauce
1/8 teaspoon sriracha
1/2 cup small cubed tofu*
Chopped scallions for garnish

Combine 1/2 of the Oriental flavor packet with the water, soy sauce and sriracha sauce, mix well and set aside

Slice the tofu into 1/2 inch cubes and set aside.

In a microwave-safe bowl break the ramen sheets into half, you will end up with 4 pieces. Pour the water mixture over the ramen, make sure all strands have been coated. Cover the bowl with microwave-safe wrap and microwave for 3 minutes. Remove the bowl from oven, unwrap the bowl, (reserve the wrap) with 2 forks separate the ramen strands. Add the tofu, recover and microwave for 90 seconds. Remove the bowl from oven, DO NOT UNCOVER, let the bowl stand, covered, for 2 to 3 minutes. Uncover and serve in a bowl topped with the poached egg and a sprinkling of chopped scallions.

*Store the left-over Tofu in a zip-lock bag, refrigerate, do not store longer than 3 days, use in Pad Thai With Tofu or Udon Ramen.

Hot N' Sour Ramen

1 package of ramen (discard the flavor packet)
1 1/2 cup water
1 teaspoon soy sauce
3 tablespoon catchup
1/2 teaspoon sriracha sauce
1/4 teaspoon sesame oil
1 teaspoon sugar
1 tablespoon rice wine vinegar
*1/2 teaspoon powdered ginger or 1 inch of
    candied ginger thinly sliced*
1/4 teaspoon garlic powder
2 teaspoon cornstarch or flour
1 egg beaten
1/2 cup tofu sliced into 1/2 inch cubes
1/4 cup chopped frozen or fresh spinach*
1/4 cup canned bamboo shoots** sliced into thin strips
1/4 cup canned straw mushrooms***
Sliced scallions for garnish

Combine the water, soy sauce, catchup, sriracha sauce, sesame oil, sugar, vinegar, ginger and garlic, mix well and set aside.

In a separate container, beat the egg until frothy, make sure the yolk is well incorporated and set aside.

Run cold water over the frozen spinach to separate the leaves, squeeze dry, and set aside.

In a microwavable bowl, break the ramen sheets in half, you will end up with 4 pieces, sprinkle flour or cornstarch over ramen, pour the water mixture over the ramen, make sure all the ramen has been coated. Cover the bowl with →

microwave-safe wrap, microwave for 3 minutes, remove the bowl from the oven, uncover, (reserve the wrap) with 2 forks separate the ramen strands. Add the tofu, spinach, bamboo shoots and mushrooms, stir well and slowly add the egg, mix just to incorporate. Recover and microwave for 90 seconds. Remove the bowl from the oven, DO NOT UNCOVER, let the bowl stand for 2 minutes. Uncover and serve.

Garnish with a sprinkling of scallions.

*Reseal the bag of frozen spinach, keep frozen and reserve to use in Greek Egg Drop Soup
**Store the left-over bamboo shoots in a zip-lock bag, refrigerate, do not store longer than 3 days, use in Pad Thai or Asian dishes.
***Store the left-over mushrooms in a zip-lock bag, refrigerate, do not store longer than 3 days, use in Pad Thai , Chop Suey or any of the Asian dishes.

California Egg Drop Soup

1 Oriental Flavor Ramen
1/2 flavor packet
1 1/2 cup water
1/2 teaspoon sesame oil
1 teaspoon rice wine vinegar
1 egg
1 cup diced tomato* (canned or fresh)

Combine the water, 1/2 of the flavor packet, the sesame oil and vinegar, mix well and set aside.

Whisk the egg until it's frothy and set aside.

In a microwavable bowl, break the ramen sheets in half, you will end up with 4 pieces. Pour the water mixture over the ramen, make sure all the ramen has been coated. Cover the bowl with microwave-safe wrap, microwave for 3 minutes, remove the bowl from the oven, uncover, (reserve the wrap) with 2 forks separate the ramen strands. Add the tomatoes, stir the soup and slowly pour the egg a tablespoon at a time into the soup, DO NOT MIX, Recover the bowl, microwave 90 seconds. Remove the bowl from the oven, DO NOT UNCOVER, let the bowl stand, covered, 2 minutes. Uncover and serve.

*Seal the tomatoes in a zip-lock bag. Reserve for use in Ramen Marinara or Ramen Primavera

Udon With Beef Jerky

1 package Oriental Flavor Ramen
1 1/2 cup Water
1 teaspoon soy sauce
1/2 package flavor packet
1 tablespoon dried onion flakes
1/4 teaspoon sesame oil
2/3 Slices of beef* or pork jerky
1/4 cup water
Scallions chopped for garnish

Rehydrate the meat in 1/4 cup water for 20 minutes. (longer is better) and set aside.

Combine the water, soy sauce, 1/2 package of the flavor packet, the onion and sesame oil, mix well and set aside.

In a microwave-safe bowl break the ramen sheets in half, you should end up with 4 pieces. Pour the water mixture over the ramen, make sure all the ramen has been coated. Cover the bowl with microwave-safe wrap and microwave for 3 minutes. Remove the bowl from oven, remove the wrap, (reserve the wrap) with 2 forks separate the ramen strands. Add the rehydrated meat slices, recover the bowl with the reserved wrap, microwave for 90 seconds. Remove the bowl from the oven, DO NOT UNCOVER, let the bowl stand, covered, for 2 to 3 minutes. Uncover and serve.

Garnish with a sprinkling of scallions.

*Reseal the bag of beef jerky, reserve and use in Tomato Beef Ramen or as a snack.

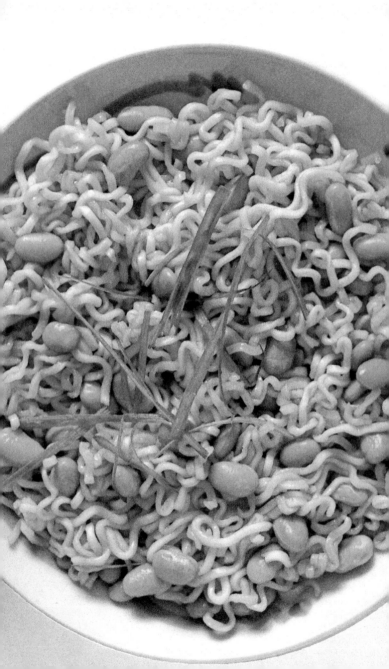

Ramen With Edamame

1 package of ramen (discard the flavor packet)
3/4 cup water
1 tablespoon + 1 teaspoon Oyster sauce**
1/4 teaspoon sesame oil
1/2 teaspoon ginger or 1 inch square of candied ginger
*   sliced into very thin strips*
1 teaspoon sugar
1/2 teaspoon cornstarch or flour
1 cup frozen edamame*
Chopped scallions for garnish

Combine the water, oyster sauce, sesame oil, ginger and sugar. Mix well and set aside.

Run cold water over the frozen edamame to remove frost, do not defrost and set aside.

In a microwave-safe bowl, break the ramen sheets in half, you will end up with 4 pieces, sprinkle with cornstarch or flour. Pour the water mixture over the ramen, make sure all the ramen has been coated. Cover the bowl with microwave-safe wrap, microwave for 2 minutes, remove the bowl from the oven, uncover, (reserve the wrap) with 2 forks separate the ramen strands. Add the edamame, recover and microwave for 90 seconds. Remove the bowl from the oven, DO NOT UNCOVER, let the bowl stand, covered, for 3 minutes. Uncover and serve.

Garnish with scallions.

*Reseal the bag to keep excess moisture out of the bag and
store frozen for use in Ramen with Bacos and Edamame.
**Use the oyster sauce in Ramen with Snow Peas & Snow Peas

Tamago Udon Ramen

TAMAGO (OMELET)

2 eggs
1 teaspoon cornstarch or flour
1/2 teaspoon soy sauce
1 tablespoon water
1 teaspoon sugar
1 teaspoon butter
A 6x6 inch microwave-safe container

Coat the container with butter and set aside.

Combine cornstarch or flour, soy sauce, water and sugar, mix well and set aside. Whisk the eggs until frothy add soy sauce water mixture, mix well. Pour into the buttered microwave-safe container (a 6 x 6 inch pan or a small square Zip-lock container). Cover with microwave-safe wrap leaving a corner uncovered to allow steam to escape. Microwave at medium heat 1 minute, remove wrap, mix and re-cover, leaving a corner uncovered, microwave 1 minute, or check every 30 seconds for doneness. Turn eggs on cutting board slice 3 long slices 1 inch thick x 4 inches long, reserve the slices, set aside. Slice the remaining omelet into 1/2 inch pieces, set aside.

THE SOUP

1 package of Oriental flavor ramen
1/2 of the flavor packet
1 1/2 cup water
1 tablespoon dried onion flakes
Scallions sliced into 3 inch long by 1/8 inch wide strips.

Combine the water, 1/2 of the flavor packet and the onion, mix well and set aside.

In a microwave-safe bowl, break the ramen sheets in half, you will end up with 4 pieces. Pour the mixture over the ramen, make sure all the ramen has been coated. Cover the bowl with microwave-safe wrap, microwave for 3 minutes. Remove the bowl from oven, uncover, (reserve the wrap) with 2 forks separate the ramen strands. Recover the bowl and microwave 90 seconds. Remove the bowl from the oven, DO NOT UNCOVER, let the bowl stand 2 minutes. Uncover, add the diced eggs, stir only to incorporate. Pour into a bowl and top with the reserved omelet slices and sprinkle with scallions.

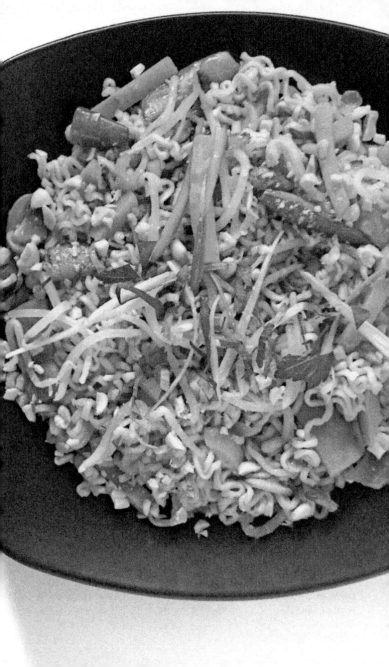

Pad Thai Ramen

1 package of ramen (discard the flavor packet)
3/4 cup water
2 tablespoon sugar
1 tablespoon peanut butter*
1 teaspoon soy sauce
1/2 teaspoon sriracha sauce
1/4 teaspoon garlic powder
1/4 teaspoon powdered ginger or 1 inch piece of
    thinly sliced candied ginger
1 1/2 cup frozen stir fry vegetables**
1/4 cup left-over canned drained bean sprouts*** or
    1/4 cup fresh sprouts
Scallions sliced into 3 inch long, 1/8 inch wide strips

Combine the water, sugar, peanut butter, soy sauce, sriracha sauce, garlic and ginger, mix well and set aside.

Run cold water over the frozen vegetables to remove frost, do not defrost, drain, add the drained bean sprouts and set aside.

In a microwave-safe bowl break the ramen sheets in half, you should end up with 4 pieces. Pour the reserved water mixture over ramen, make sure all the ramen has been coated. Cover the bowl with microwave-safe wrap, microwave for 2 minutes. Remove the bowl from the oven, uncover the bowl, (reserve the wrap) with 2 forks separate the ramen strands. Add the vegetables, cover, microwave for 90 seconds. Remove the bowl from the oven, DO NOT UNCOVER, let the bowl stand, covered, for 2 to 3 minutes. Uncover, mix to incorporate and serve.

Garnish with scallions.

*The Peanut butter can be used in the following recipes, Peanut Ramen and Dan Dan Ramen
**Reseal the bag of frozen stir fried vegetables, keep frozen and reserve to use in Chop Suey or Chowramen.
***Store the left-over bean sprouts in a zip-lock bag, store refrigerated for up to 4 days, reserve for use in Pad Thai With Tofu and any of the Asian dishes.

Pad Thai Ramen With Tofu

1 package of ramen (discard the flavor packet)
3/4 cup water
1 tablespoon sugar
1 teaspoon oyster sauce
1/4 teaspoon sriracha sauce
1/4 teaspoon garlic powder
1/4 teaspoon powdered ginger or a 1 inch piece of candied
*   ginger sliced into thin slices*
1 egg
1/2 cup Tofu* sliced into 1/4 x 1/4 x 2 inch long strips
1/2 cup sliced bamboo shoots
Scallions slivered into 4 inch long slices 1/8 inch thick

In a cup combine the water, sugar, oyster sauce, sriracha sauce, garlic and ginger, mix well and set aside.

In a separate container, with a fork, beat the egg until frothy and set aside.

In a microwave-safe bowl break the ramen sheets in to half, you should end up with 4 pieces. Pour the water mixture over the ramen, make sure all the ramen has been coated with the mixture. Cover the bowl with microwave-safe wrap, microwave for 2 minutes. Remove the bowl from the oven, uncover the bowl (reserve the wrap) with 2 forks separate the ramen strands. Add the tofu and bamboo shoots, mix well, stirring slowly add egg one tablespoon at a time (do not mix). Recover the bowl and microwave for 90 seconds. Remove the bowl from the oven, DO NOT UNCOVER, let the bowl stand, covered, for 2 to 3 minutes. Uncover and serve.

Garnish with scallions.

*Store the left-over Tofu in a zip-lock bag, refrigerate, do not store longer than 3 days, use in Udon with Poached Egg and Tofu.

Red Curry Soup

1 package of ramen (discard the flavor packet)
1/2 cup water
1/2 teaspoon dried ginger or 1 inch crystallized ginger, diced
1/4 teaspoon powdered garlic
1 teaspoon sugar
1 cup cocoanut milk*
1+ 1/2 teaspoon red curry paste**
1/2 cup frozen spinach***or 1 cup fresh spinach
1 tablespoon lime juice
Scallions slivered in 1/8 inch strands 4 inches long for garnish

Combine the water, ginger, garlic and sugar, mix well, and set aside.

Run water over the frozen spinach to eliminate frost, squeeze dry, set aside.

Combine the curry paste and cocoanut milk, mix well and set aside.

In a microwavable bowl, break the ramen sheets in half, you will end up with 4 pieces. Pour the water mixture over the ramen, make sure all the ramen has been coated. Cover the bowl with microwave-safe wrap, microwave for 2 minutes. Remove the bowl from the oven, uncover, (reserve the wrap) with 2 forks separate the ramen strands. Pour cocoanut milk curry mixture over the ramen, add spinach mix to incorporate, recover and microwave for 2 minutes. Remove the bowl from the oven, DO NOT UNCOVER, let the bowl stand, covered, for 3 minutes. Uncover and serve.

Drizzle with lime juice and garnish with scallions.

*Store the cocoanut milk in a clean jar, refrigerate, do not store longer than 3 days, use in Tai Curry or Cocoanut Banana Pudding.
**Use in Tai Curry
***Store the frozen spinach in a zip-lock bag, keep frozen for use in Frittata, Greek Egg Drop Soup or Cannellini Ramen Soup

Udon Ramen

1 package of Oriental flavor ramen
1/2 flavor packet
1 1/2 cup water
1/4 teaspoon sriracha sauce
1 teaspoon soy sauce
1/2 teaspoon sugar
1/2 cup Tofu* (optional)
Scallions

Combine the water, 1/2 of the Oriental flavor packet, the soy sauce, sugar and sriracha sauce, mix well and set aside

Slice the tofu into 1/2 inch cubes and set aside.

In a microwave-safe bowl break the ramen sheets into half, you will end up with 4 pieces. Pour the water mixture over the ramen, make sure all the ramen has been coated. Cover the bowl with microwave-safe wrap and microwave for 3 minutes. Remove the bowl from the oven, unwrap the bowl, (reserve the wrap) with 2 forks separate the ramen strands. Add the tofu, re-wrap the bowl and microwave for 90 seconds. Remove the bowl from oven. DO NOT UNCOVER, let the bowl stand, covered, for 2 minutes. Uncover and serve.

Garnish with a sprinkling of scallions.

*Store the left-over Tofu in a zip-lock bag, refrigerate, do not store longer than 3 days, use in Pad Thai With Tofu or Udon With Poached Egg.

Tai Curry Ramen

1 package Ramen, (discard the flavor packet)
1 cup coconut milk* (you can substitute water,
  but it's not as good)
1 tablespoon Tai Red Curry or 2 teaspoon curry powder
2 teaspoon sugar
2 tablespoon raisins
2 cup frozen California style vegetables**
1 tablespoon butter
1 teaspoon parsley or cilantro
Coconut flakes

Place the frozen vegetables in a microwavable bowl, cover with microwave-safe wrap, microwave for 90 seconds. Remove the bowl from oven, unwrap the bowl (reserve the wrap) stir, recover the and set aside.

Combine the curry, sugar, raisins and coconut milk, mix well and set aside.

In a microwave-safe bowl break the ramen sheets in half, you will end up with 4 pieces. Pour the coconut mixture over noodles, make sure all the ramen has been coated, micro-wave 2 minutes, uncover the bowl and (reserve the wrap) using 2 forks separate the ramen strands. Add 1 tablespoon butter, cover, and microwave for 1 minute. Remove the bowl from the oven and let stand, covered, for 2 minutes. Unwrap the bowl, (reserve wrap) add the vegetables, mix only to blend, re-wrap bowl microwave 1 to 2 minutes. Remove the bowl from the oven, DO NOT UNCOVER, let the bowl stand 2 minutes. Uncover and serve.

Garnish with a sprinkling of chopped parsley, cilantro or coconut flakes.

*Store the left-over coconut milk in a clean jar and reserve to use in Curry Soup.
**Reseal the bag of frozen vegetables, keep frozen and reserve to use in Veggie Ramen Soup or Curry Soup.

2 Egg Drop Soup

1 package chicken flavor Ramen
1 1/2 cup water
1/2 flavor packet
1/2 teaspoon powdered ginger or
*   1 inch of candied ginger sliced into thin strips*
1 tablespoon lime juice
1/4 teaspoon sriracha sauce
1 teaspoon cornstarch or flour
2 eggs, lightly beaten
Scallions

Combine the water, 1/2 of the flavor packet, the ginger, lime juice and sriracha sauce, mix well and set aside.

In a small container lightly beat the eggs and set aside.

In a microwavable bowl, break the ramen sheets in half, you will end up with 4 pieces, sprinkle the flour or cornstarch over the ramen, pour the water mixture over the ramen, make sure all the ramen has been coated. Cover the bowl with microwave-safe wrap, microwave for 3 minutes, remove the bowl from the oven, uncover the bowl, (reserve the wrap) with 2 forks separate the ramen strands. Slowly stir the soup in circular motion, slowly pour the eggs into soup, do not over mix. Recover the bowl, microwave for 2 minutes. Remove the bowl from the oven, DO NOT UNCOVER, let the bowl stand, covered, for 2 minutes. Uncover and serve.

Garnish with sliced lime and scallions.

Chocolate Ramen

1 package of ramen, (discard the flavor packet)
1/2 of the ramen noodles
1/2 cup water
2 tablespoon milk (or 2 containers of Half & Half
   from the cafeteria)
1 tablespoon cocoa
1 egg
1 egg yoke
2 tablespoon sugar (6 packets from the cafeteria)
1/4 teaspoon salt
1 teaspoon vanilla
1 teaspoon of melted butter (1 pad from the cafeteria)
Chocolate syrup (optional)
Redi whip or Cool Whip (optional)

Use one half of a butter pad to butter a 2 cup microwave-safe container (I use Zip-lock) and set aside.

Combine the water, milk and cocoa, mix well and set aside.

Beat the eggs until frothy, add sugar and salt beat well, set aside. In a separate container, melt the butter and set aside.

Break the ramen sheets in half, you will have 2 sheets, place one sheet into a bag, with a can or hammer, lightly pound the bag to break-up the ramen into rice size pieces. Pour the ramen into a microwave-safe bowl, add the water mixture, ramen should be coated, soak the ramen for 10 minutes or longer, stir the ramen 2 or 3 times. Cover the bowl with microwave-safe wrap, microwave 2 minutes, remove the bowl from the oven, uncover the bowl, (reserve the wrap) stir the ramen and set aside.

Combine the egg, sugar and vanilla, whisk until pale yellow, add the melted butter, mix well and pour over ramen, mix together well. Pour into the buttered container, cover with reserved wrap, microwave 3 minutes. Remove the container from the oven, DO NOT UNCOVER, let the container stand, covered, to cool.

To serve, place serving plate over the cooled pudding, flip to release. Drizzle with chocolate syrup and top with whipped cream or cool whip.

Strawberry Delite

1 package of ramen, (discard the flavor packet)
1/2 of package of ramen noodles
1/2 cup water
2 tablespoon milk (2 containers of Half & Half from the
*   cafeteria)*
3 tablespoon strawberry syrup (Nesquick)
2 eggs
1 tablespoon sugar
1/4 teaspoon salt
1 teaspoon vanilla
1 teaspoon of melted butter (1 pad from the cafeteria)
1 cup frozen or fresh strawberries (optional)
Rediwhip (optional)

Use one half of a butter pad to butter a 2 cup micro-wave-safe container (I use Zip-lock) and set aside.

Combine water, milk and strawberry syrup, mix well, set aside.

Beat the egg until frothy, add the sugar and salt, beat well and set aside. In a separate container, melt butter and set aside.

Break the ramen sheets in half, you will have 2 sheets, place one sheet into bag, with a can or hammer, lightly pound the bag to break-up the ramen into rice size pieces. Pour the ramen into a microwave-safe bowl, add the water mixture and mix, ramen should be coated, let stand 10 minutes or longer, stir the ramen 2 or 3 times during the soak. Cover the bowl with microwave-safe wrap, microwave 2 minutes. Remove the bowl from the oven, uncover the container, (reserve wrap) stir and set aside.

Slice the strawberries into quarters and add to the ramen. Reserve 1 strawberry for garnish

Combine the egg mixture and vanilla, whisk until pale yellow and frothy, slowly add the melted butter, mix well and pour over ramen, mix well. Pour mixture into the buttered container. Cover the container with reserved wrap, microwave 3 minutes. Remove the container from the oven, DO NOT UNCOVER, let the container stand, covered, to cool. Uncover and serve or refrigerate for later use.

To serve, place serving plate over cooled pudding, flip to release pudding drizzle with strawberry syrup and top with whip cream or cool whip and the reserved strawberry, sliced.

Coconut Banana Pudding

1 package of ramen, (discard the flavor packet)
3/4 cup cocoanut milk*
1/4 teaspoon cinnamon
1 inch square ginger, diced
1/2 teaspoon salt
1/4 cup raisins
1 tablespoon butter (2 pads from the cafeteria)
1 egg
2 tablespoon sugar
2 tablespoon sour cream
1 teaspoon vanilla
1 banana sliced into 1/4 inch rounds
Shredded cocoanut (optional)**

Use one half of a butter pad to butter a 2 cup micro-wave-safe container (I use Zip-lock) and set aside.

In a bowl combine the cocoanut milk, cinnamon, ginger, raisins and salt, mix well and set aside.

Melt the 1 1/2 pads of butter and set aside.

Break the ramen sheets in half, you will have 2 sheets, place one sheet into a bag, lightly pound the bag with a can or hammer, break-up the ramen into rice size pieces. Pour the ramen into a microwave-safe container, add cocoanut milk mixture, coat the ramen, stir ramen 2 or 3 times. Soak the ramen for 10+ minutes. Cover the container with microwave-safe wrap, microwave for 2 minutes. Remove the container from the oven, uncover, (reserve the wrap) stir the ramen, and set aside.

Slice the bananas, carefully add the bananas to the ramen, reserve 3 or 4 slices for garnish, set aside.

Beat the egg and add sugar, beat until frothy, add sour cream, vanilla and the melted butter, whisk well, add to the ramen, mix well. Pour the mixture into the reserved container, cover with micro-wave-safe wrap, microwave 3 minutes. Remove the container from the oven, DO NOT UNCOVER, let the container stand, covered, to cool. The pudding can be refrigerated and served cold.

To serve, place serving plate over cooled pudding, flip to release pudding. Garnish with sliced bananas and shredded cocoanut.

*Store the left-over coconut milk in a clean jar, store refrigerated for up to 4 days. Can be used in Curry Ramen or Pad Thai peanut
**Reseal the bag of coconut. Can be used in Tai Curry

Lemon Curd Ramen

1 package of ramen, (discard the flavor packet)
3/4 cup water
1/4 teaspoon grated lemon rind
1 egg (beat till frothy)
2 to 3 tablespoon lemon juice
2 tablespoon sugar
1 tablespoon of melted butter (2 pads from the cafeteria)
Redi Whip or Cool Whip

Use one half of a butter pad to butter a 2 cup microwave-safe container (I use Zip-lock) and set aside.

Break the ramen sheets in half, you will have 2 sheets, place one sheet into a bag, lightly pound the bag with a can or hammer, break-up the ramen into rice size pieces. Pour the ramen into a microwave-safe container, combine the ramen and water, mix well. Let the mixture soak 10 minutes and stir the ramen well. Cover the container with microwave-safe wrap and microwave 2 minutes. Remove the container from oven, uncover and stir, recover and set aside..

In a small bowl beat the egg until frothy, add the sugar, lemon rind, lemon juice and melted butter, whisk until frothy. Add the egg-lemon mixture to the ramen, mix well, make sure the egg-lemon mixture is totally incorporated. Pour the mixture into the buttered container. Cover the container with micro-wave-safe wrap and microwave 2 minutes. Remove the container from the oven, DO NOT UNCOVER, let the container stand, covered, to cool. Uncover and serve. The pudding can be refrigerated and served cold.

To serve, place a plate over the container and flip. Serve with whip cream or Redi Whip.

This book is also
available digitally for
Nook, Kindle and iBooks and
readers in mobi
or epub formats.

Visit your favorite
online store
to order.